A Family Guide to the Biblical Feasts

CeLeBRaTinG JeSuS
through the
FeaSTS of ISRaeL

Wyatt House books may be ordered through booksellers or by contacting:

WYATT HOUSE PUBLISHING
399 Lakeview Dr. W.
Mobile, Alabama 36695
www.wyattpublishing.com
editor@wyattpublishing.com

Because of the dynamic nature of the Internet, any web address or links contained in this book may have changed since publication and may no longer be valid.

Cover design by: Sam Noerr, Gyroscope

Interior design by: Mark Wyatt

ISBN 13:978-1-954798-11-3

Printed in the United States of America

A Family Guide to the Biblical Feasts

Celebrating Jesus through the Feasts of Israel

by MATT DAY

WJP

Mobile, Alabama

Dedication

To my four children and their children and their children's children...the gift of Scripture is the best gift I can ever give you. May the words of this book always be engrained in your minds and hearts, and may you constantly see Jesus as the only, perfect sacrifice for sin and the only way to the Father. Jesus loves you, and so do I, more than you will ever know!

InTRoducTioN

The 7 feasts of Israel can have a great impact on you, your family and your children if you allow them to. If you aren't familiar with these feasts, let me introduce them to you.

Israel has 7 feasts or 7 holidays that they celebrate throughout the year. They are found in Leviticus 23. God commanded the nation of Israel to keep these feasts FOREVER. For the nation of Israel, they are seen as a time of reflection. God wanted them to never forget how He miraculously rescued them from bondage in Egypt.

However, not only do these feasts look back at what has happened in the past, they also look forward to what is happening and to what will happen in the future.

These feasts are not just feasts or religious holidays. They are not manmade, man invented or man originated. These feasts are God birthed and God ordained. God said that they are His feasts, and He gave them to Israel by His sovereign wisdom, and best of all they relate to the Church today.

The central figure in all of these feasts and the fulfillment of all of these feasts is the Lord Jesus Christ. Collectively they tell a magnificent story about how God is working in our world today and what God is up to at this very hour. They are God's timeline of redemption, and God marches to the drumbeat of these feasts.

Listed below are the 7 Feasts of Israel:

- **Passover**
- **The Feast of Unleavened Bread**
- **The Feast of First Fruits**
- **The Feast of Pentecost**
- **The Feast of Trumpets**
- **The Day of Atonement**
- **The Feast of Shelters**

These feasts can be divided into two sections: Spring and Fall. There are four spring feasts (Passover, Unleavened Bread, First Fruits and Pentecost). All of these feasts have been fulfilled by Jesus.

There are three fall feasts (Trumpets, The Day of Atonement and Shelters). All of these feasts have yet to be fulfilled by Jesus. They are set in the future, and Jesus will fulfill them when the time is ready.

The purpose of this book is to be a guide for you as you celebrate these feasts as a family. In each section you will find a brief overview about each feast and a step-by-step guide on how you can tangibly celebrate that particular feast.

You might be asking yourself, *"Why is this even important?"* Here's the promise that I'm going to make to you. By choosing to creatively celebrate these feasts as a family, you will be giving your children and yourself a valuable gift—the gift of Scripture. Not only will they hear the salvation story of God year after year in an exciting, fun and creative way, they also will know that story by heart.

This book is designed to help you bridge the gap between the Old Testament and the New Testament, between Israel and the Church, and as you celebrate these feasts as a family year after year, your children will begin to know the Bible from front to back and know the beautiful story of redemption that God has woven so gracefully throughout the pages of Scripture.

1

PaSsoveR

When: Thursday and Friday of Easter Weekend.

What you will need:

- Clean the whole house
- Fine china and fine clothes
- Unleavened bread, roasted lamb, bitter herbs
- Linen napkin
- Some kind of reward
- Prince of Egypt movie

InTRoducTioN:

Read this to your children:

*But the blood on your doorposts will serve as a sign, marking the houses where you are staying. When I see the blood, **I will pass over you**. This plague of death will not touch you when I strike the land of Egypt. (Exodus 12:13 NLT)*

*Get rid of the old "yeast" by removing this wicked person from among you. Then you will be like a fresh batch of dough made without yeast, which is what you really are. **Christ, our Passover Lamb**, has been sacrificed for us. (1 Corinthians 5:7 NLT)*

The first feast that God gave to the people of Israel is the feast of Passover. It commemorates the night that God rescued Moses and the nation of Israel from bondage in Egypt. God sent 10 plagues against Pharaoh, and after the 10th plague (the killing of the firstborn in Egypt) Pharaoh finally relented, letting God's people go. On the eve of that 10th plague, God gave his people the feast of Passover.

They were to eat unleavened bread, roasted lamb and bitter herbs, all of which are very symbolic. They were to take the blood of an innocent, unblemished lamb and smear it on the sides and over the doorposts of their houses. When the death angel of God came to take the life of every firstborn, he did so only from the houses where the blood of the lamb was not applied. For every house where the blood was applied, he passed over that house. Everyone inside one of those houses was saved.

Jesus, our sinless, spotless lamb died on Passover. As the priests on Passover were lifting up the lambs to be slaughtered for the festival, Jesus died at that very moment.

PaSsoveR CeLeBRatioN

The Passover celebration can be celebrated on Easter weekend, or if you would like to look up the official calendar day of Passover, you can do that.

On **Thursday** of that week, begin preparing for the Passover celebration which will happen on Good Friday.

Traditionally in a Jewish household, there was much excitement surrounding and leading up to the Passover celebration. The children were to know that this was a very special day and that it was unlike all the other days on their calendar. Tell your children,

"Tomorrow is when we remember how God rescued Israel from slavery in Egypt, and tomorrow is when we celebrate Jesus dying on the cross for us, rescuing us from the slavery of sin."

On **Good Friday**, have everyone in your family participate in the cleaning of the home. (You can make this as extensive as you want). Jewish households would start by **cleaning the whole house**, making sure there was no yeast in it. Why is that important? Yeast in the Bible is symbolic of sin and decay. They wanted themselves and their houses to be ready and prepared to celebrate this special occasion.

Next, in preparation the Passover dinner, **pull out the fine china** and have everyone **put on their fine clothes**. (You can make this as elaborate as you want. The idea is for them to know that this is a very special event).

For the meal, you need to **serve 3 things**: *Unleavened Bread, Roasted Lamb and Bitter Herbs* (like horseradish, romaine lettuce or endive). (You can serve more than this, but these 3 pieces of food need to be included in the meal for the object lesson to be learned).

At the beginning of the meal, a game is usually played that involves 3 pieces of unleavened bread. In keeping with tradition, the middle or the 2nd piece is broken in half. It would then be wrapped in a linen napkin and hidden somewhere in the house by the father. After the meal, the children were sent to search for the hidden bread. The one who found it would then be rewarded with some **prize**.

After the meal, recall the Passover story in Exodus.

While the Israelites were still in the land of Egypt, the Lord gave the following instructions to Moses and Aaron: ² "From now on, this month will be the first month of the year for you. ³ Announce to the whole community of Israel that on the tenth day of this month each family must choose a lamb or a young goat for a sacrifice, one animal for each household. *4 If a family is too small to eat a whole animal, let them share with another family in the neighborhood. Divide the animal according to the size of each family and how much they can eat. 5 The animal you select must be a one-year-old male, either a sheep or a goat, with no defects. 6 "Take special care of this chosen animal until the evening of the fourteenth day of this first month. Then the whole assembly of the community of Israel must slaughter their lamb or young goat at twilight. 7 They are to take some of the blood and smear it on the sides and top of the doorframes of the houses where they eat the animal. 8 That same night they must roast the meat over a fire and eat it along with bitter salad greens and bread made without yeast. 9 Do not eat any of the meat raw or boiled in water. The whole animal—including the head, legs, and internal organs—must be roasted over a fire. 10 Do not leave any of it until the next morning. Burn whatever is not eaten before morning. 11 "These are your instructions for eating this meal: Be fully dressed, wear your sandals, and carry your walking stick in your hand. Eat the meal with urgency, for this is the Lord's Passover. 12 On that night I will pass through the land of Egypt and strike down every firstborn son and firstborn male animal in the land of Egypt. I will execute judgment against all the gods of Egypt, for I am the Lord!*

*¹³ But the blood on your doorposts will serve as a sign, marking the houses where you are staying. When I see the blood, I will **pass over** you. This plague of death will not touch you when I strike the land of Egypt. (Exodus 12:1-13 NLT)*

Then, discuss with your children how Jesus is the Passover Lamb. (It is really fun and impactful to act out this story with your children! Have them act it out with enthusiasm and passion).

*Now it was the governor's custom each year during the **Passover** celebration to release one prisoner to the crowd—anyone they wanted. ¹⁶ This year there was a notorious prisoner, a man named Barabbas. ¹⁷ As the crowds gathered before Pilate's house that morning, he asked them, "Which one do you want me to release to you—Barabbas, or Jesus who is called the Messiah?" ¹⁸ (He knew very well that the religious leaders had arrested Jesus out of envy.) ¹⁹ Just then, as Pilate was sitting on the judgment seat, his wife sent him this message: "Leave that innocent man alone. I suffered through a terrible nightmare about him last night." ²⁰ Meanwhile, the leading priests and the elders persuaded the crowd to ask for Barabbas to be released and for Jesus to be put to death. ²¹ So the governor asked again, "Which of these two do you want me to release to you?" The crowd shouted back, "Barabbas!" ²² Pilate* responded, "Then what should I do with Jesus who is called the Messiah?" They shouted back, "Crucify him!" [23] "Why?" Pilate demanded. "What crime has he committed?" But the mob roared even louder, "Crucify him!" [24] Pilate saw that he wasn't getting anywhere and that a riot was developing. So he sent for a bowl of water and washed his hands before the crowd, saying, "I am innocent of this man's blood. The responsibility is yours!" [25] And all the people yelled back, "We will take responsibility for his death—we and our children!" [26] So Pilate released Barabbas to them. He ordered Jesus flogged with a lead-tipped whip, then turned him over to the Roman soldiers to be crucified. [27] Some of the governor's soldiers took Jesus into their headquarters and called out the entire regiment. [28] They stripped him and put a scarlet robe on him. [29] They wove thorn branches into a crown and put it on his head, and they placed a reed stick in his right hand as a scepter. Then they knelt before him in mockery and taunted, "Hail! King of the Jews!" [30] And they spit on him and grabbed the stick and struck him on the head with it. [31] When they were finally tired of mocking him, they took off the robe and put his own clothes on him again. Then they led him away to be crucified.

[45] At noon, darkness fell across the whole land until three o'clock. [46] At about three o'clock, Jesus called out with a loud voice, "Eli, Eli, lema sabachthani?" which means

"My God, my God, why have you abandoned me?" ⁴⁷
*Some of the bystanders misunderstood and thought he
was calling for the prophet Elijah. ⁴⁸ One of them ran
and filled a sponge with sour wine, holding it up to him
on a reed stick so he could drink. ⁴⁹ But the rest said,
"Wait! Let's see whether Elijah comes to save him." ⁵⁰
Then Jesus shouted out again, and he released his spirit. ⁵¹ At that moment the curtain in the sanctuary of the
Temple was torn in two, from top to bottom. The earth
shook, rocks split apart, ⁵² and tombs opened. The bodies of many godly men and women who had died were
raised from the dead. ⁵³ They left the cemetery after Jesus' resurrection, went into the holy city of Jerusalem,
and appeared to many people.⁵⁴ The Roman officer and
the other soldiers at the crucifixion were terrified by the
earthquake and all that had happened. They said, "This
man truly was the Son of God!" (Matt. 27:15-32,45-54
NLT)*

Next, talk about how this relates to Jesus today. (Have
everyone participating take turns reading the Scriptures).

God Rescues Us From Slavery

Everyone of us are trapped or were trapped in the world's
system. The world's system is Egypt, the world's king is
the devil, and the world's taskmaster is sin.

Once you were dead because of your disobedience and your many sins. ² You used to live in sin, just like the rest of the world, obeying the devil—the commander of the powers in the unseen world. He is the spirit at work in the hearts of those who refuse to obey God. ³ All of us used to live that way, following the passionate desires and inclinations of our sinful nature. By our very nature we were subject to God's anger, just like everyone else. (Ephesians 2:1-3 NLT)

We know that our old sinful selves were crucified with Christ so that sin might lose its power in our lives. We are no longer slaves to sin. ⁷ For when we died with Christ we were set free from the power of sin. (Romans 6:6-7 NLT)

Just as God rescued his people out of slavery in Egypt, He rescues all who will come to Him out of the clutches of the world, the flesh, and the devil.

Jesus Is The Lamb

He was oppressed and treated harshly, yet he never said a word. He was led like a lamb to the slaughter. And as a sheep is silent before the shearers, he did not open his mouth.⁸ Unjustly condemned, he was led away. (Isaiah 53:7-8 NLT)

The next day John saw Jesus coming toward him and said, "Look! The Lamb of God who takes away the sin of the world! [30] *He is the one I was talking about when I said, 'A man is coming after me who is far greater than I am, for he existed long before me.' (John 1:29-30 NLT)*

And they sang in a mighty chorus: "Worthy is the Lamb who was slaughtered—to receive power and riches and wisdom and strength and honor and glory and blessing." [13] *And then I heard every creature in heaven and on earth and under the earth and in the sea. They sang: "Blessing and honor and glory and power belong to the one sitting on the throne and to the Lamb forever and ever."* [14] *And the four living beings said, "Amen!" And the twenty-four elders fell down and worshiped the Lamb. (Revelation 5:12-14 NLT)*

The Lamb Was Without Blemish

It had to be a perfect sacrifice.

For God made Christ, who never sinned, to be the offering for our sin, so that we could be made right with God through Christ. (2 Corinthians 5:21 NLT)

The Lamb Was Killed And Its Blood Was Smeared On The Door

For you know that God paid a ransom to save you from the empty life you inherited from your ancestors. And the ransom he paid was not mere gold or silver. ¹⁹ It was the precious blood of Christ, the sinless, spotless Lamb of God. ²⁰ God chose him as your ransom long before the world began, but he has now revealed him to you in these last days. (1 Peter 1:18-20 NLT)

The Power of Egypt Was Destroyed

So the people of Israel did just as the Lord had commanded through Moses and Aaron. ²⁹ And that night at midnight, the Lord struck down all the firstborn sons in the land of Egypt, from the firstborn son of Pharaoh, who sat on his throne, to the firstborn son of the prisoner in the dungeon. Even the firstborn of their livestock were killed. ³⁰ Pharaoh and all his officials and all the people of Egypt woke up during the night, and loud wailing was heard throughout the land of Egypt. There was not a single house where someone had not died. ³¹ Pharaoh sent for Moses and Aaron during the night. "Get out!" he ordered. "Leave my people—and take the rest of the Israelites with you! Go and worship the Lord as you have requested." (Exodus 12:28-31 NLT)

In the same way that the power of Egypt was destroyed, through the death of Jesus the power of sin and death was completely destroyed for those who trust in His sacrifice.

You were dead because of your sins and because your sinful nature was not yet cut away. Then God made you alive with Christ, for he forgave all our sins. [14] He canceled the record of the charges against us and took it away by nailing it to the cross. [15] In this way, he disarmed the spiritual rulers and authorities. He shamed them publicly by his victory over them on the cross. (Colossians 2:13-15 NLT)

Next, explain to your children what they ate at the Passover Meal.

Explain eating the **lamb** by saying, *"We ate lamb to remember that Jesus is our Passover Lamb that was sacrificed on our behalf for our sin."*

Explain eating the **bitter herbs** by saying, *"We ate bitter herbs to remind us of the life of sin that we were once enslaved to. God rescued us from that life and we never want to return to it."*

Explain eating the **unleavened bread** by saying, *"We ate unleavened bread to remember that Jesus was without sin, just as we should always be without sin as we present our bodies to God."*

After the acting out of the story and the explanation, send the children to find the hidden bread and then reward the one who finds it (Actually, reward all of them if you have more than one child unless you want a fight on your hands. You can reward the one who found it just a little bit more if you would like).

When the hidden bread has been found, **explain the meaning of the ceremony.**

The Trinity (God the Father, God the Son, God the Holy Spirit) is represented in the 3 pieces of bread.

- The 2nd person of the Trinity (Jesus) was broken for our sin.

- He was wrapped in a linen sheet (buried)

- He was resurrected (found) on the 3rd day.

- There is a reward for all who find Him (salvation)

Conclude this special time by praying and thanking God for the sacrifice of His Precious Son.

Finish the time, after all the dishes have been put away, by watching together as a family *The Prince of Egypt* movie. Not only does it show the Exodus out of Egypt and all that was involved in that, it also has great music!

Throughout the weekend or as they go to bed, make time to talk with your children about what they experienced and heard during the Passover celebration. Talk with them about their salvation. If they know the Lord, rejoice with them in that. If they don't, gently push open that door and talk with them about it.

2

The Feast of Unleavened Bread

When: Saturday of Easter Weekend

What you will need:

- Unleavened bread (tortillas)

- Leavened bread (sandwich bread)

- Plastic eggs

- Candy

InTRoducTioN:

Read this to your children.

"The Lord's Passover begins at sundown on the four-teenth day of the first month. ⁶ On the next day, the fif-teenth day of the month, you must begin celebrating the Festival of Unleavened Bread. This festival to the Lord continues for seven days, and during that time the bread you eat must be made without yeast. (Leviticus 23:5-6 NLT)

Get rid of the old "yeast" by removing this wicked person from among you. Then you will be like a fresh batch of dough made without yeast, which is what you real-ly are. Christ, our Passover Lamb, has been sacrificed for us. ⁸ So let us celebrate the festival, not with the old bread of wickedness and evil, but with the new bread of sincerity and truth. (1 Corinthians 5:7-8)

The next feast, The Feast of Unleavened Bread, hap-pened the very next day after Passover, and it lasted for 7 days. No yeast was to be found anywhere in their com-munity.

Its meaning is rooted within the Exodus story (Exodus 12). When God told Moses to prepare to leave Egypt, they were to eat the Passover meal with urgency being fully dressed with all of their bags packed. They were to eat unleavened bread (bread with no yeast in it) because they didn't have time to let the bread rise. God was about to deliver them from slavery quickly. For this reason, God told Israel to always celebrate this festival— for it was with speed that the Lord delivered His people.

Why was yeast used as the object lesson? It has a dual meaning.

(1) **It was a reminder to them of the swift nature of their delivery**

God did not delay. He was faithful to His promise. He delivered them with speed.

(2) **It was a reminder to them to consecrate themselves as holy unto the Lord**

God had sovereignly brought them out of Egypt. They were His holy people. He was to be their holy God.

Yeast, all throughout the Bible is representative of sin, and for good reasons. Yeast is a fungus. It rapidly permeates the dough, contaminates it, sours it, and swells it to many times its original size without changing its weight. It is a small thing that spreads secretly and quietly, and yeast decays things... just like sin.

This is why the Bible uses it as a metaphor for sin. So, as they were ridding their homes of yeast, they were to be rededicating themselves to God.

How does this relate to Jesus? Jesus was in the ground on the Feast of Unleavened Bread. If Passover points to the cross, Unleavened Bread points to the grave that was occupied by Jesus. But, how did He occupy it? He occupied it as One who was without sin and One who was about to be speedily resurrected.

UnLeavened BReaD CeLeBRation

On Easter weekend, you can celebrate the Feast of Unleavened Bread as a family on Saturday, the day before Easter.

Unleavened Bread Eating Contest—At some point on Saturday, have an Unleavened Bread eating contest. Give each of your children a piece of unleavened bread (tortilla), and let them race to see who can eat it the fastest.

When it's all done, explain how yeast is a picture of sin and how God delivered Jesus out of the grave quickly because He had no sin.

Say to them, *"Jesus was a pure, sinless (without leaven) sacrifice."*

Take turns reading these Scriptures, before playing the hide and seek game that night.

He was oppressed and treated harshly, yet he never said a word. He was led like a lamb to the slaughter. And as a sheep is silent before the shearers, he did not open his mouth. ⁸ Unjustly condemned, he was led away. No one cared that he died without descendants, that his life was cut short in midstream. But he was struck down for the rebellion of my people. ⁹ He had done no wrong and had never deceived anyone. But he was buried like a criminal; he was put in a rich man's grave. (Isaiah 53:7-9 NLT)

So then, since we have a great High Priest who has entered heaven, Jesus the Son of God, let us hold firmly to what we believe. ¹⁵ This High Priest of ours understands our weaknesses, for he faced all of the same testings we do, yet he did not sin. (Hebrews 4:14-15 NLT)

Say to them, *"Because Jesus had no sin, God raised Him with speed. His body was not permitted to decay in the tomb."*

"People of Israel, listen! God publicly endorsed Jesus the Nazarene by doing powerful miracles, wonders, and signs through him, as you well know. ²³ But God knew what would happen, and his prearranged plan was carried out when Jesus was betrayed. With the help of lawless Gentiles, you nailed him to a cross and killed him. ²⁴ But God released him from the horrors of death and raised him back to life, for death could not keep him in its grip. ²⁵ King David said this about him: 'I see that the Lord is always with me. I will not be shaken, for he is right beside me. ²⁶ No wonder my heart is glad, and my tongue shouts his praises! My body rests

in hope. ²⁷ *For you will not leave my soul among the dead or allow your Holy One to rot in the grave.* ²⁸ *You have shown me the way of life, and you will fill me with the joy of your presence.'*

²⁹ *"Dear brothers, think about this! You can be sure that the patriarch David wasn't referring to himself, for he died and was buried, and his tomb is still here among us.* ³⁰ *But he was a prophet, and he knew God had promised with an oath that one of David's own descendants would sit on his throne.* ³¹ *David was looking into the future and speaking of the Messiah's resurrection. He was saying that God would not leave him among the dead or allow his body to rot in the grave.* ³² *"God raised Jesus from the dead, and we are all witnesses of this.* ³³ *Now he is exalted to the place of highest honor in heaven, at God's right hand. And the Father, as he had promised, gave him the Holy Spirit to pour out upon us, just as you see and hear today." (Acts 2:22-33 NLT)*

Leaven Hide and Seek Game—Saturday night play the leaven hide and seek game.

Here's how you play it. In Jewish households, after all the leaven was removed from the house, the mother would permit the children to go through the house and place leaven in certain hiding places. With all the lights out in the house, the father would light a candle and begin his search for the leaven with the children following closely behind him. Even though it was a fun game, they made sure all the leaven was taken outside of the house. It was a reminder to them that sin must be constantly searched out and removed as we live before a Holy God.

How you can play it today:

Take Easter eggs and fill some of them with leavened bread (bread with yeast in it) **and some with candy.** Parents will hide the eggs all throughout the house for the kids to find. Turn out all the lights in the house, make it as dark as you can, arm your kids with flashlights and baskets and let them loose!

When all the eggs are found, sort them. Put all of the candy in one spot and all the leavened bread in another.

Take the leavened bread outside. Put the leavened bread in a pile outside and burn the bread in a safe environment, away from the house and under parental supervision.

While everyone is sitting around the burning bread, explain to them what they are learning.

Talk with them about sin. Ask them to explain to you what sin is. Ask them to list out for you some deeds that they believe are sinful.

Tell them the reason for the hide and seek game.
"The bread inside the eggs represents sin in our life. Just as the eggs with bread were searched for and removed from the house, the same should be done with our lives. We ought to make sure all of the time that all of the sin is completely out of us."

Tell them why you are burning the yeast. *"Just as we have taken this leaven outside and are burning it, let us remember how Jesus carried our sins away for us and faced the fire of God's judgment and wrath on our behalf."*

While the fire is burning talk about the fire in relationship to Jesus. Everything that Jesus experienced on the cross, the wrath of God, the punishment from God, the alienation from God is all represented by the fire. God put the fire of His wrath on his Son so that we don't have to. It cost Him His very life. How then should we look at sin? How can we look at sin in a flippant way?

When the fire is almost out, ask your children to take an inventory of their sin. Is there anything in their life or your life that is unpleasing to the Lord? When that time is finished, pray with your children. Thank God for the forgiveness that He offers in Jesus and the fact that we don't have to live in slavery to sin any longer.

3
The Feast of
FIRST FRuiTS

When: Easter Sunday

What you will need:

- Empty Tomb rolls

- Easter Sunday meal

- Resurrection place settings

InfRoducTioN:

Read this to your children:

*Then the Lord said to Moses, 10 "Give the following in-structions to the people of Israel. When you enter the land I am giving you and you harvest its **first** crops, bring the priest a bundle of grain from the **first** cutting of your grain harvest." (Leviticus 23:9-10 NLT)*

*But in fact, Christ has been raised from the dead. He is the **first** of a great harvest of all who have died. (1 Corinthians 15:20 NLT)*

This festival happened the day after the Sabbath which would put it being celebrated on a Sunday (the day Jesus rose from the dead). This is the time in the nation of Israel of harvesting the barley grain. It was filled with a sense of great expectation like we view Christmas morning today.

Months before the grain was harvested, the nation of Israel as a whole and each individual family was to ear-mark a bundle or a portion of their grain and designate it as their first-fruit offering. As far as the family was concerned, fathers, along with their children, would find the best section of their grain, take a rope and section it off.

When the Feast of First Fruits drew near, fathers, with their skipping children following behind them, would go out to the field and cut the first fruit section. They would then take their grain portion to Jerusalem and present it to the priest. The priest upon receiving it would wave it before the Lord symbolically saying *"God, you gave this to us, we are now giving it back to you."* God was so serious about the first fruits offering that He commanded that the rest of the harvest back home was not to be used until the first portion was given to Him.

Jesus rose on First Fruits. As all of these grain offerings were being waved before the Lord by the priest, the resurrected Christ was the first harvest being waved before the Lord saying, *"I AM alive forevermore, and I'm the first of a great harvest that is yet to come!"*

This is why it says in Matthew 27:

Then Jesus shouted out again, and he released his spirit. 51 At that moment the curtain in the sanctuary of the Temple was torn in two, from top to bottom. The earth shook, rocks split apart, 52 and tombs opened. The bodies of many godly men and women who had died were raised from the dead. 53 They left the cemetery after Jesus' resurrection, went into the holy city of Jerusalem, and appeared to many people. (Matthew 27: 50-53 NLT)

What was the point of people rising from their graves at the crucifixion and leaving the cemetery AFTER Jesus' resurrection? Jesus presented His first-fruit portion to the Lord as a testimony, a guarantee that there is a greater of harvest of souls to come!

FIRSt FRuiTS CeLeBRatioN

Good Friday is the Passover celebration. Saturday is the celebration of Unleavened Bread. **Easter Sunday** is the day you can celebrate the Feast of First Fruits (the Resurrection of Jesus from the dead).

Empty Tomb Rolls—for breakfast make "Empty Tomb Rolls" or "Resurrection Buns." These are crescent rolls wrapped around a marshmallow. When you bake them in the oven, the marshmallow melts leaving a hollow, empty space in the middle (just like an empty tomb!). When each child bites into their roll, they are to say clearly and loudly, *"He is not here. He is risen!"*

Look online to find out how to make these delicious treats

Easter Sunday Meal—Easter Sunday meals are typically large in general. Try to include grains, veggies and fruit (things from a harvest) in your meal in order to represent the harvest.

Resurrection Place Settings—In preparation for the meal, put a Scripture in front of everyone's plate. Write the Scripture on a 3x5 blank index card and fold it in half. It can either be a Scripture about Jesus' resurrection or our eventual resurrection as Christ-followers.

Have everyone present read the Scripture placed before them at some point during the meal.

During the meal, explain what the Feast of First Fruits is about. Take turns reading these Scriptures:

*Then the Lord said to Moses, ¹⁰ "Give the following instructions to the people of Israel. When you enter the land I am giving you and you harvest its first crops, bring the priest a bundle of grain from the first cutting of your grain harvest. ¹¹ On the day after the Sabbath, the priest will lift it up before the **Lord** so it may be accepted on your behalf. ¹⁴ Do not eat any bread or roasted grain or fresh kernels on that day until you bring this offering to your God. This is a permanent law for you, and it must be observed from generation to generation wherever you live. (Leviticus 23:9-11, 14 NLT)*

Talk about how Jesus rose from the dead on this feast.

But very early on Sunday morning the women went to the tomb, taking the spices they had prepared. ² They found that the stone had been rolled away from the entrance. ³ So they went in, but they didn't find the body of the Lord Jesus. ⁴ As they stood there puzzled, two men suddenly appeared to them, clothed in dazzling robes. ⁵ The women were terrified and bowed with their faces to the ground. Then the men asked, "Why are you looking among the dead for someone who is alive? ⁶ He isn't here! He is risen from the dead! Remember what he told you back in Galilee, [7] that the Son of Man must be betrayed into the hands of sinful men and be crucified, and that he would rise again on the third day." (Luke 24:1-7 NLT)

Next, read about **our** resurrection.

*But tell me this—since we preach that Christ rose from the dead, why are some of you saying there will be no resurrection of the dead? [13] For if there is no resurrection of the dead, then Christ has not been raised either. [14] And if Christ has not been raised, then all our preaching is useless, and your faith is useless. [15] And we apostles would all be lying about God—for we have said that God raised Christ from the grave. But that can't be true if there is no resurrection of the dead. [16] And if there is no resurrection of the dead, then Christ has not been raised. [17] And if Christ has not been raised, then your faith is useless and you are still guilty of your sins. [18] In that case, all who have died believing in Christ are lost! [19] And if our hope in Christ is only for this life, we are more to be pitied than anyone in the world. [20] **But in fact, Christ has been raised from the dead. He is the first of a great harvest of all who have died.** [21] So you see, just as death came into the world through a man, now the resurrection from the dead has begun through another man. [22] Just as everyone dies because* *we all belong to Adam, everyone who belongs to Christ will be given new life. ²³ But there is an order to this resurrection: Christ was raised as the first of the harvest; then all who belong to Christ will be raised when he comes back. (1 Corinthians 15:12-23 NLT)*

Lastly, talk about how we are to always give our best to God. Our first fruits, not our leftovers.

Let the message about Christ, in all its richness, fill your lives. Teach and counsel each other with all the wisdom he gives. Sing psalms and hymns and spiritual songs to God with thankful hearts. ¹⁷ And whatever you do or say, do it as a representative of the Lord Jesus, giving thanks through him to God the Father. (Colossians 3:16-17 NLT)

Just as the best portion of the harvest was to be dedicated to God, so too our lives should be representative of that harvest dedication every single day as we live on this earth in preparation for our eventual resurrection.

4

The Feast of Pentecost

When: A Friday night, Saturday night and Sunday night, six weeks after Easter.

What you will need:

- Coffee
- Lots of sweets

InTRoduCTioN:

Read this to your children:

*"From the day after the Sabbath—the day you bring the bundle of grain to be lifted up as a special offering—count off seven full weeks. ¹⁶ Keep counting until the day after the seventh Sabbath, **fifty days later**. Then present an offering of new grain to the Lord." (Leviticus 23:15-16 NLT)*

*On the day of **Pentecost** all the believers were meeting together in one place. ² Suddenly, there was a sound from heaven like the roaring of a mighty windstorm, and it filled the house where they were sitting. (Acts 2:1-2 NLT)*

The Greek name for "fifty" is "pentecost." The reason it is called the Feast of Pentecost is because this festival occurred exactly 50 days after the Feast of First Fruits. It was one of three "solemn" feasts out of the 7 Feasts of Israel, which meant that during these specific feasts (First Fruits, Pentecost, and Shelters), every man had to present himself to the Lord at the Temple in Jerusalem. By the way, this is why on the day of Pentecost when the Holy Spirit came as told in the book of Acts, there were people from all over the known world gathered there. They were there to appear before the Lord and the priest at the Temple.

What was its purpose? The same process that occurred for First Fruits occurred for this festival. They were to journey to Jerusalem and appear before the priests with an offering of wheat this time instead of barley. Just like before, the rest of the harvest back home could not be touched until this offering was made. But, here's what was different about this offering.

Instead of bringing a bundle of grain to the priest like they did at First Fruits, they were now to bring two loaves of bread. The interesting thing about these two loaves is that they were to be made WITH YEAST! Remember what yeast represents? Sin and decay, yet God was telling them now that yeast had to be put back into this offering. Here's why.

When the Holy Spirit came at Pentecost in the book of Acts, He came to both Jews and Gentiles thus representing the two loaves of bread. Just like the yeast in those loaves of bread, what was once removed (yeast and Gentiles) was now being put back in (yeast and Gentiles). Gentiles were now included in God's gift of salvation. Praise God for that!

One other thing that began to occur on this feast that dates back to even before the birth of Jesus is that they would read Scriptures from the book of Habakkuk and Ezekiel about the powerful, earth shattering presence of

God. Later on, in Ezekiel, the glory of God departed from the Temple because of sin within the nation of Israel.

Every Feast of Pentecost they would pray for God's presence to return to the Temple, and they believed that on this day, the day of Pentecost, the glorious presence of God would return to the Temple once again! Isn't that amazing? It's no accident that God chose this day of all days to powerfully descend upon mankind in the person of the Holy Spirit, not to dwell in manmade temples, but within the hearts of men.

PentecoSt CeLeBRatioN

Set aside a weekend about 6 weeks after Easter for 3 nights of celebration!

Friday night:

Celebrate The Giving of God's Word

Jews believe that this is the time that God gave the 10 Commandments (the Law) to the people of Israel and to Moses on Mount Sinai. They spend time thanking God for His Law, and they spend time reading His Law. They make this a very fun time by eating sweets like cheesecake and such. They do this to remind themselves that the Law is sweet like milk and honey. They also stay up all night eating sweets, drinking coffee, and reading the Law.

The Bible is so important to us, and I believe we should spend time celebrating it as well.

- During this evening, talk about the importance of the Bible and how we should read it and obey it.

- Eat sweet stuff (cheesecake, ice cream, brownies) and explain to your kids why they are eating this way. Say to them, *"We are eating these sweets be-cause the Word is sweet like milk and honey."*

- Stay up late into the night or even all night and read from and discuss the Word. Eat sweets, drink coffee and have a blast taking in the Word of God!

Saturday night:

Celebrate the Coming of the Holy Spirit

- Read excerpts from the passages that were read every Pentecost in Ezekiel and Habakkuk that talk about the awesome presence of God. (Take turns reading these Scriptures).

As I looked, I saw a great storm coming from the north, driving before it a huge cloud that flashed with light-ning and shone with brilliant light. There was fire inside the cloud, and in the middle of the fire glowed something like gleaming amber.

Then the Spirit lifted me up, and I heard a loud rum-bling sound behind me. (May the glory of the Lord be praised in his place!) (Ezekiel 1:4 and 3:12 NLT)

I see God moving across the deserts from Edom, the Holy One coming from Mount Paran. His brilliant splendor fills the heavens, and the earth is filled with his praise. ⁴ His coming is as brilliant as the sunrise. Rays of light flash from his hands, where his awesome power is hidden. ⁵ Pestilence marches before him; plague follows close behind.⁶ When he stops, the earth shakes. When he looks, the nations tremble. He shatters the everlasting mountains and levels the eternal hills. He is the Eternal One! (Habakkuk 3:3-6 NLT)

This is what they were reading when the Holy Spirit came at Pentecost!

- Read from Acts 2 about the coming of the Holy Spirit

On the day of Pentecost all the believers were meeting together in one place. ² Suddenly, there was a sound from heaven like the roaring of a mighty windstorm, and it filled the house where they were sitting. ³ Then, what looked like flames or tongues of fire appeared and settled on each of them. ⁴ And everyone present was filled with the Holy Spirit and began speaking in other languages, as the Holy Spirit gave them this ability.

⁵ At that time there were devout Jews from every nation living in Jerusalem. ⁶ When they heard the loud noise, everyone came running, and they were bewildered to hear their own languages being spoken by the believers.⁷ They were completely amazed. "How can this be?" they exclaimed. "These people are all from Galilee, ⁸ and yet we hear them speaking in our own native languages!

[12] *They stood there amazed and perplexed. "What can this mean?" they asked each other.* [13] *But others in the crowd ridiculed them, saying, "They're just drunk, that's all!"* [14] *Then Peter stepped forward with the eleven other apostles and shouted to the crowd, "Listen carefully, all of you, fellow Jews and residents of Jerusalem! Make no mistake about this.* [15] *These people are not drunk, as some of you are assuming. Nine o'clock in the morning is much too early for that.* [16] *No, what you see was predicted long ago by the prophet Joel:* [17] *'In the last days,' God says, 'I will pour out my Spirit upon all people. Your sons and daughters will prophesy. Your young men will see visions, and your old men will dream dreams.* [18] *In those days I will pour out my Spirit even on my servants—men and women alike—and they will prophesy.* [19] *And I will cause wonders in the heavens above and signs on the earth below—blood and fire and clouds of smoke.* [20] *The sun will become dark, and the moon will turn blood red before that great and glorious day of the Lord arrives.* [21] *But everyone who calls on the name of the Lord will be saved.'* [22] *"People of Israel, listen! God publicly endorsed Jesus the Nazarene by doing powerful miracles, wonders, and signs through him, as you well know.* [23] *But God knew what would happen, and his prearranged plan was carried out when Jesus was betrayed. With the help of lawless Gentiles, you nailed him to a cross and killed him.* [24] *But God released him*

from the horrors of death and raised him back to life, for death could not keep him in its grip.

"God raised Jesus from the dead, and we are all witnesses of this. 33 Now he is exalted to the place of highest honor in heaven, at God's right hand. And the Father, as he had promised, gave him the Holy Spirit to pour out upon us, just as you see and hear today. 34 For David himself never ascended into heaven, yet he said, 'The Lord said to my Lord, "Sit in the place of honor at my right hand 35 until I humble your enemies, making them a footstool under your feet."' 36 "So let everyone in Israel know for certain that God has made this Jesus, whom you crucified, to be both Lord and Messiah!" 37 Peter's words pierced their hearts, and they said to him and to the other apostles, "Brothers, what should we do?" 38 Peter replied, "Each of you must repent of your sins and turn to God, and be baptized in the name of Jesus Christ for the forgiveness of your sins. Then you will receive the gift of the Holy Spirit. 39 This promise is to you, and to your children, and even to the Gentiles—all who have been called by the Lord our God." 40 Then Peter continued preaching for a long time, strongly urging all his listeners, "Save yourselves from this crooked generation!" 41 Those who believed what Peter said were baptized and added to the church that day—about 3,000 in all. (Acts 2:1-8,12-24,32-41 NLT)

Discuss what is happening in this passage. Ask your children to tell you what the people witnessing this event might have been feeling at that time.

- Read from John 14 and John 16 the words of Jesus about the Holy Spirit

"If you love me, obey my commandments. ¹⁶ And I will ask the Father, and he will give you another Advocate, who will never leave you. ¹⁷ He is the Holy Spirit, who leads into all truth. The world cannot receive him, because it isn't looking for him and doesn't recognize him. But you know him, because he lives with you now and later will be in you. (John 14:15-17 NLT)

"But now I am going away to the one who sent me, and not one of you is asking where I am going.

⁶ Instead, you grieve because of what I've told you. ⁷ But in fact, it is best for you that I go away, because if I don't, the Advocate won't come. If I do go away, then I will send him to you. ⁸ And when he comes, he will convict the world of its sin, and of God's righteousness, and of the coming judgment. ⁹ The world's sin is that it refuses to believe in me. ¹⁰ Righteousness is available because I go to the Father, and you will see me no more. ¹¹ Judgment will come because the ruler of this world has already been judged.

[12] *"There is so much more I want to tell you, but you can't bear it now. [13] When the Spirit of truth comes, he will guide you into all truth. He will not speak on his own but will tell you what he has heard. He will tell you about the future. [14] He will bring me glory by telling you whatever he receives from me. [15] All that belongs to the Father is mine; this is why I said, 'The Spirit will tell you whatever he receives from me.' (John 16:5-15 NLT)*

Ask your children, *"What do these passages say about the Holy Spirit? How does the Bible describe Him?"*

Next, read about the power and presence of the Holy Spirit in the life of a believer.

Don't you realize that your body is the temple of the Holy Spirit, who lives in you and was given to you by God? You do not belong to yourself, [20] for God bought you with a high price. So you must honor God with your body. (1 Corinthians 6:19-20 NLT)

My old self has been crucified with Christ. It is no longer I who live, but Christ lives in me. So I live in this earthly body by trusting in the Son of God, who loved me and gave himself for me. (Galatians 2:20 NLT).

So I say, let the Holy Spirit guide your lives. Then you won't be doing what your sinful nature craves. [17] The sinful nature wants to do evil, which is just the opposite of what the Spirit wants. And the Spirit gives us desires that are the opposite of what the sinful nature desires. These two forces are constantly fighting each other, so you are not free to carry out your good intentions. ¹⁸But when you are directed by the Spirit, you are not under obligation to the law of Moses. ¹⁹When you follow the desires of your sinful nature, the results are very clear: sexual immorality, impurity, lustful pleasures, ²⁰idolatry, sorcery, hostility, quarreling, jealousy, outbursts of anger, selfish ambition, dissension, division, ²¹envy, drunkenness, wild parties, and other sins like these. Let me tell you again, as I have before, that anyone living that sort of life will not inherit the Kingdom of God. ²² But the Holy Spirit produces this kind of fruit in our lives: love, joy, peace, patience, kindness, goodness, faithfulness, ²³gentleness, and self-control. There is no law against these things! ²⁴Those who belong to Christ Jesus have nailed the passions and desires of their sinful nature to his cross and crucified them there. ²⁵Since we are living by the Spirit, let us follow the Spirit's leading in every part of our lives. (Galatians 5:16-25 NLT)

Ask your children to describe the role of the Holy Spirit in a believer's life.

- Eat sweets during this time to remember that the Holy Spirit has come to live inside our hearts. Say to your children, *"We are eating sweets because the Holy Spirit is the sweet gift of God."*

Sunday:

Celebrate the birth of the Church

- Gather with your church body

- Read in Acts 2 about how the church should function (Take turns reading these Scriptures)

All the believers devoted themselves to the apostles' teaching, and to fellowship, and to sharing in meals (including the Lord's Supper), and to prayer. [43] A deep sense of awe came over them all, and the apostles performed many miraculous signs and wonders. [44] And all the believers met together in one place and shared everything they had. [45] They sold their property and possessions and shared the money with those in need. [46] They worshiped together at the Temple each day, met in homes for the Lord's Supper, and shared their meals with great joy and generosity— [47] all the while praising God and enjoying the goodwill of all the people. And each day the Lord added to their fellowship those who were being saved. (Acts 2:42-47 NLT)

- Read in Ephesians 2 about how everyone who comes to Christ is welcomed into God's family.

But now you have been united with Christ Jesus. Once you were far away from God, but now you have been brought near to him through the blood of Christ. [14] For

Christ himself has brought peace to us. He united Jews and Gentiles into one people when, in his own body on the cross, he broke down the wall of hostility that separated us. 15 He did this by ending the system of law with its commandments and regulations. He made peace between Jews and Gentiles by creating in himself one new people from the two groups. 16 Together as one body, Christ reconciled both groups to God by means of his death on the cross, and our hostility toward each other was put to death. (Ephesians 2:13-16 NLT)

- Eat leavened bread to demonstrate the unity we have in God's family as Jews and Gentiles.

- Eat sweets because of the sweet fellowship that we share as the body of Christ.

Say to your children, *"We are eating sweets because of the sweet fellowship that we have with one another in the body of Christ."*

Conclude this time by:

- Praying for the salvation of Israel that they would come to Jesus as Savior and Lord.

- Praying for the salvation of the people around you who do not know God.

5
The FeaSt of TRumpetS

When: Some time in September or October before the new moon appears. (You can look that up online).

What you will need:

- Instruments that make noise

- Apples dipped in honey

- A new article of clothing for each person

InrRoducTioN:

Read this to your children.

Give the following instructions to the people of Israel. On the first day of the appointed month in early autumn, you are to observe a day of complete rest. It will be an official day for holy assembly, a day commemorated with loud blasts of a **trumpet**. *(Leviticus 23:24 NLT)*

For the Lord himself will come down from heaven with a commanding shout, with the voice of the archangel, and with the **trumpet** *call of God. First, the Christians who have died will rise from their graves. (1 Thessalonians 4:16 NLT)*

The Feast of Trumpets is a very unique feast for several reasons. It is the first of the fall feasts occurring sometime in September or October. The previous feast, The Feast of Pentecost, happens some 3 months before this feast. By the time this feast rolls around, the people are quite anxious. It has been a long wait for them, and they are ready for another feast of the Lord.

Secondly, it commemorates no event in Israel's past that we specifically know of. On this feast, they were to offer some of the usual sacrifices as the other feasts, and they were to observe it as a day of rest just like most of the other feasts. However, here's what's interesting. They were to primarily observe this day as a day of blowing trumpets. Sounds a little weird, doesn't it? Rest and blow trumpets? It does until you realize WHEN it occurs on the calendar and in the month.

The Feast of Trumpets is the only feast to occur on the first day of the month. Now, why is that important? If you remember, the Jewish calendar is a lunar calendar. When the new moon appears, that's when their month starts. So not only did this feast involve a time of waiting, it also involved a time of watching. As soon as the first presence of the moon appeared, they would start the festival...by blowing trumpets. It involved waiting, it involved watching, and it involved blowing a trumpet to signal the time.

Does that sound like familiar language to the New Testament church? It should! It all points to Jesus, His return, and our eventual resurrection as we watch for and expectantly wait for the sound of God's trumpet!

TRumpetS CeLeBRatioN

The Feast of Trumpets is celebrated sometime in the fall around September or October, and it begins when the new moon appears. Jewish fathers would take their children out at night around the time of this feast and look up to the sky to see if they could see the moon. When they saw it, they would blow a trumpet. That sounds like a good tradition to me!

Plan ahead of time as to when the new moon will appear. Again, you can look that up online.

Go out for a few days before the moon appears with your children. Ask them, *"Do you see the moon yet?"* After they spend some time searching for it, say to them, *"Maybe it will be tomorrow night."*

On the night that the moon appears, celebrate it by having everybody blow an instrument at the same time (kazoo, bugle, whistle, trumpet, whatever). Make it a celebratory time, and make it loud. Then, explain to them the meaning of what they are doing.

Tell them that a trumpet will signal the return of Jesus. Take turns reading the Scriptures.

But let me reveal to you a wonderful secret. We will not all die, but we will all be transformed! [52] *It will happen in a moment, in the blink of an eye, when the last trumpet is blown. For when the trumpet sounds, those who have died will be raised to live forever. And we who are living will also be transformed. (1 Corinthians 15:51-52 NLT)*

We tell you this directly from the Lord: We who are still living when the Lord returns will not meet him ahead of those who have died. [16] For the Lord himself will come down from heaven with a commanding shout, with the voice of the archangel, and with the trumpet call of God. First, the Christians who have died will rise from their graves. [17] Then, together with them, we who are still alive and remain on the earth will be caught up in the clouds to meet the Lord in the air. Then we will be with the Lord forever. [18] So encourage each other with these words. (1Thessalonians 4:15-18 NLT)

And then at last, the sign that the Son of Man is coming will appear in the heavens, and there will be deep mourning among all the peoples of the earth. And they will see the Son of Man coming on the clouds of heaven with power and great glory. [31] And he will send out his angels with the mighty blast of a trumpet, and they will gather his chosen ones from all over the world—from the farthest ends of the earth and heaven. (Matthew 24:30-31 NLT)

Talk about the reality and the surety of Jesus' return. Ask them what they think that day will look like.

The Jewish people during this feast would often eat apples dipped in honey. **Eat** apples dipped in honey to remind everyone of the sweetness of eternity.

Talk with them about how we will receive new bodies.

Take turns reading these Scriptures:

But we are citizens of heaven, where the Lord Jesus Christ lives. And we are eagerly waiting for him to return as our Savior. 21 He will take our weak mortal bodies and change them into glorious bodies like his own, using the same power with which he will bring everything under his control. (Philippians 3:20-21 NLT)

It is the same way with the resurrection of the dead. Our earthly bodies are planted in the ground when we die, but they will be raised to live forever. 43 Our bodies are buried in brokenness, but they will be raised in glory. They are buried in weakness, but they will be raised in strength. 44 They are buried as natural human bodies, but they will be raised as spiritual bodies. For just as there are natural bodies, there are also spiritual bodies. 45 The Scriptures tell us, "The first man, Adam, became a living person." But the last Adam—that is, Christ—is a life-giving Spirit. 46 What comes first is the natural body, then the spiritual body comes later. 47 Adam, the first man, was made from the dust of the earth, while Christ, the second man, came from heaven. 48 Earthly people are like the earthly man, and heavenly people are like the heavenly man. 49 Just as we are now like the earthly man, we will someday be like the heavenly man. (1 Corinthians 15:42-49 NLT)

- Imagine with your children about what our heavenly bodies might look like and be able to do. Ask them what they think their new body will look like and what it might be able to do.

- **Buy** a new outfit or piece of clothing for everyone symbolizing how our bodies and garments will change. Give it to them now or at the end of the feast.

In the timeline of God, according to the feasts, we are living in the Pentecostal Age. The Holy Spirit has come, and He dwells within the heart of every true child of God. We are living right now in between the Day of Pentecost and the Day of Christ's return signaled by the sound of a trumpet!

Are we close to the Day of Trumpets, when Jesus comes back? We are closer today than we have ever been before! What events going on right now let you know that we are close?

How should we be living and what should we be doing while we wait for the Lord's return?

- In our waiting, we are to be working for the Lord, doing His will

- In our working, we are to be witnessing, telling others about Jesus and His love

- In our watching, we are to be ready

Take turns reading these Scriptures:

"When the Son of Man returns, it will be like it was in Noah's day. 38 In those days before the flood, the people were enjoying banquets and parties and weddings right up to the time Noah entered his boat. 39 People didn't realize what was going to happen until the flood came and swept them all away. That is the way it will be when the Son of Man comes. 40 "Two men will be working together in the field; one will be taken, the other left. 41 Two women will be grinding flour at the mill; one will be taken, the other left. 42 "So you, too, must keep watch! For you don't know what day your Lord is coming. 43 Understand this: If a homeowner knew exactly when a burglar was coming, he would keep watch and not permit his house to be broken into. 44 You also must be ready all the time, for the Son of Man will come when least expected. (Matthew 24:37-44 NLT)

But you aren't in the dark about these things, dear brothers and sisters, and you won't be surprised when the day of the Lord comes like a thief. ⁵ For you are all children of the light and of the day; we don't belong to darkness and night. ⁶ So be on your guard, not asleep like the others. Stay alert and be clearheaded. (1 Thessalonians 5:4-6 NLT)

Close with this story:

Pastor and Author Francis Chan used a long rope to illustrate the difference between our time on this earth versus our time in eternity.

On the very end of the rope, he covered about six inches of the rope with red tape. The rest of the rope, which stretched across the full stage of the auditorium, was left bare.

This was his point. The 6-inch taped part of the rope represents the length of our existence on this earth. The un-taped portion of the rope, represents eternity.

We spend so much time and energy living for the little piece of existence that we know on earth, and yet we don't consider the perspective of eternity.

Ask your family to wrestle with these questions.

"Am I ready for the return of Jesus?"

"Would I be ashamed if He came back today?"

"What do I need to do in light of His coming?"

"How should I be living my life in light of eternity?"

- Pray together as a family.

- Lead your family in praying for people without Christ—for those you know and for people throughout the world.

6

The Day of Atonement

What you will need:

- Talk with your children ahead of time about fasting at some point during this feast.

- Bread and water for the evening meal.

IntRoducTioN:

Read this to your children.

For the life of a creature is in the blood, and I have given it to you to make **atonement** *for yourselves on the altar; it is the blood that makes* **atonement** *for one's life. (Leviticus 17:11 NIV)*

Just think how much more the blood of Christ will purify our consciences from sinful deeds so that we can worship the living God. For by the power of the eternal Spirit, Christ offered himself to God as a perfect sacrifice for our sins. (Hebrews 9:14 NLT)

The Day of Atonement is the holiest Jewish day on the calendar. It is the day of "atoning" or "covering" the sins of the people for the previous year. It was a very sobering and somber day characterized by deep inward reflection, soul searching and **fasting**. This is the day that the High Priest would enter the Holy of Holies (the place in the Temple where the presence of God dwelt), and stand and minister in the very presence of God. He could only go in once a year, and He could only go in on this day.

In order for the High Priest to stand in the presence of God and not die, he had to follow God's special precautions: like washing multiple times before entering, wearing the right garments, burning the incense that preceded him into the Holy Place, and entering with the blood offering from an innocent animal sacrifice. In order for a guilty people to be pardoned, something innocent had to die and take their place. That was true for them then, and it's true for us now.

This was such a High and Holy day in Israel that God commanded special sacrifices to be made on top of all the other usual sacrifices. Here's what would happen. As the priest stood before the people, a bull was presented to him. He pressed his two hands upon the forehead of the bull (confessing his sins and transferring them to the bull).

Next, he turned his attention to the two goats standing before him that were identical in size, identical in color and identical in value. There were two names in a bowl. YHWH (the Holy Name of God) and the name for the word "Scapegoat." He would take the names out and hold them over the forehead of each animal. The one that had the name "scapegoat" over it was immediately identified and a crimson strip of wool was tied to one of its horns. It waited there, before the people, until all the other sacrifices were completed. The other goat was sacrificed to the Lord on the altar.

The bull that waited there was then used. The High Priest pressed his hands on the animal once again, placing the sins of the priesthood on the animal. It also was sacrificed to the Lord. Next, he would take that blood and the blood of the goat into the Holy of Holies and sprinkle all of that blood over everything (the Ark of the Covenant, the walls, the veil that separated the Holy of Holies, etc).

Lastly, he would return to the scapegoat. He laid his hands on the forehead of that animal and transferred the sin of the people onto it. The scapegoat was then taken out of the city, led away, never to be seen again symbolizing that God had removed their sins from them, at least for one more year.

This celebration is all about blood, and it is the blood of Jesus, the sinless, spotless Lamb of God, who eternally covers those who are trusting in Him.

Atonement Celebration

The Day of Atonement happens 9 days after the Feast of Trumpets. Pick a day around then that works for your schedule, and celebrate it as a very holy, reflective day.

It is customary to eat differently during the celebration of this feast, remembering that we will all stand before Christ to be judged. During our evening meal, we observe this holy, somber and reflective time as a family by **eating bread and drinking water**.

After you read the Day of Atonement overview in this booklet to your family, explain to your children who Jesus is in the story. Take turns reading the Scriptures.

Jesus Is The High Priest

So Christ has now become the High Priest over all the good things that have come. He has entered that greater, more perfect Tabernacle in heaven, which was not made by human hands and is not part of this created world. (Hebrews 9:11 NLT)

Jesus Is The Sacrifice At The Altar

For by the power of the eternal Spirit, Christ offered

himself to God as a perfect sacrifice for our sins. [15] That is why he is the one who mediates a new covenant between God and people, so that all who are called can receive the eternal inheritance God has promised them. For Christ died to set them free from the penalty of the sins they had committed under that first covenant. (Hebrews 9:14a-15 NLT)

Jesus Is The YHWH Goat

For a child is born to us, a son is given to us. The government will rest on his shoulders. And he will be called: Wonderful Counselor, Mighty God, Everlasting Father, Prince of Peace. (Isaiah 9:6 NLT)

In the beginning was the Word, and the Word was with God, and the Word was God.

The Word became flesh and made his dwelling among us. We have seen his glory, the glory of the one and only Son, who came from the Father, full of grace and truth. (John 1:1,14 NIV)

For Christ also suffered once for sins, the righteous for the unrighteous, to bring you to God. He was put to death in the body but made alive in the Spirit. (1 Peter 3:18, NIV)

Jesus Is The Blood

With his own blood—not the blood of goats and calves— he entered the Most Holy Place once for all time and secured our redemption forever. Under the old system, the blood of goats and bulls and the ashes of a young cow could cleanse people's bodies from ceremonial impurity. ¹⁴ Just think how much more the blood of Christ will purify our consciences from sinful deeds so that we can worship the living God. (Hebrews 9:12-14a NLT)

Jesus Is The Scapegoat

Yet it was our weaknesses he carried; it was our sorrows that weighed him down. And we thought his troubles were a punishment from God, a punishment for his own sins! ⁵ But he was pierced for our rebellion, crushed for our sins. He was beaten so we could be whole. He was whipped so we could be healed. ⁶ All of us, like sheep, have strayed away. We have left God's paths to follow our own. Yet the Lord laid on him the sins of us all. (Isaiah 53:4-6 NLT)

The next day John saw Jesus coming toward him and said, "Look! The Lamb of God who takes away the sin of the world! (John 1:29 NLT)

Talk about how this feast relates to us now.

*And so, dear brothers and sisters, we can **boldly enter** heaven's Most Holy Place because of the blood of Jesus. [20] By his death, Jesus opened a new and life-giving way through the curtain into the Most Holy Place. [21] And since we have a great High Priest who rules over God's house, [22] **let us go right into the presence of God** with sincere hearts fully trusting him. For our guilty consciences have been sprinkled with Christ's blood to make us clean, and our bodies have been washed with pure water. (Hebrews 10:19-22 NLT)*

Say to your children: *"It means that if we've taken part in Passover (applying the blood and trusting in the blood) we are forever covered by the blood of Jesus. There is no more payment required. Unlike the High Priest who could only go into the presence of God once a year, and only enter with the offering of the blood from an innocent animal, we now have complete, unhindered access to the Father because of the perpetual blood of Christ. The curtain is torn, the payment for sin has been taken care of by the cross forever, and the guilt and burden of sin has been removed forever."*

Then, turn your attention to how this feast relates to the future. Tell your children, *"This will be the time that we stand before the judgment seat of God after the trumpet has sounded."*

And I saw a great white throne and the one sitting on it. The earth and sky fled from his presence, but they found no place to hide. 12 I saw the dead, both great and small, standing before God's throne. And the books were opened, including the Book of Life. And the dead were judged according to what they had done, as recorded in the books. 13 The sea gave up its dead, and death and the grave gave up their dead. And all were judged according to their deeds. 14 Then death and the grave were thrown into the lake of fire. This lake of fire is the second death. 15 And anyone whose name was not found recorded in the Book of Life was thrown into the lake of fire. (Revelation 20:11-15 NLT)

Explain to them that we, as followers of Jesus, are not to be judged for our sins. We are forever covered or "atoned" by the blood of Jesus. Our judgment will be a judgment to determine the rewards each Christ-follower will receive.

For no one can lay any foundation other than the one we already have—Jesus Christ. 12 Anyone who builds on that foundation may use a variety of materials— gold, silver, jewels, wood, hay, or straw. 13 But on the judgment day, fire will reveal what kind of work each builder has done. The fire will show if a person's work has any value. 14 If the work survives, that builder will receive a reward. 15 But if the work is burned up, the builder will suffer great loss. The builder will be saved, but like someone barely escaping through a wall of flames. (1 Corinthians 3:11-15 NLT)

We will be rewarded based on:

- How faithfully we served Christ

- How well we obeyed the Great Commission call to evangelize

- How victorious we were over sin

- How well we controlled our tongues, and the list could go on.

Discuss with each other for what else we might be rewarded.

Ask your children, *"Why was the Day of Atonement a day of dread and terror for the people of Israel during this time?"*

After they've answered, tell them, *"This will also be a dreadful time for us as all people will stand before God."*

He will wipe every tear from their eyes, and there will be no more death or sorrow or crying or pain. All these things are gone forever." (Revelation 21:4 NLT)

Do you know when this wiping away of tears occurs? It occurs in Heaven.

Ask them, *"Why would there be a need to wipe away every tear in Heaven?"*

Here's the answer:

"Because, this wiping away of tears happens right after the final judgement. There will be tears shed on the day of judgement, because there will be great sorrow as we see the people that we know, cast away from God forever. They will look at us and ask us, "You knew about this offering of salvation? Why didn't you tell me?" There will be great sorrow in our hearts as we watch them be cast into the Lake of Fire for all eternity.

There will also be great sorrow for us to realize that we wasted our lives living for the kingdom of this world rather than for the Kingdom of God."

It is after this time of weeping that God will then wipe away every tear from our eyes.

Realize that day is coming! Make sure your family knows that this time of judgement will definitely come.

"This is why we fast as we reflect on this somber, dreadful and mournful day."

Talk with them about their salvation.

Pray with them about others and their friends who do not know God.

Pray for the salvation of Israel, that they might escape this day of judgement by believing in Jesus as Messiah.

7

The Feast of Shelters

When: A weekend night about 5 days after the Day of Atonement

What you will need:

- Tent

- Everyone's favorite foods (Make a list, go to the store and buy all of it!)

- Gifts for your children (think Christmas!)

InTRoducTioN:

Read this to your children.

For seven days you must live outside in little **shelters**. *All native-born Israelites must live in* **shelters**. *43 This will remind each new generation of Israelites that I made their ancestors live in* **shelters** *when I rescued them from the land of Egypt. I am the Lord your God."* *(Leviticus 23:42-43 NLT)*

The Word became flesh and **made his dwelling among us**. *We have seen his glory, the glory of the one and only Son, who came from the Father, full of grace and truth. (John 1:14 NIV)*

And I heard a loud voice from the throne saying, "Look! **God's dwelling place is now among the people**, *and he will dwell with them. They will be his people, and God himself will be with them and be their God. (Revelation 21:3 NIV)*

Israel's last feast and most joyous feast is the Feast of Shelters which occurs 5 days after the Day of Atonement. It was also the last of Israel's 3 solemn feasts, where every man had to travel to Jerusalem, appear before the Lord at the Temple, and present gifts to Him.

As sojourners from all over the region made their way to Jerusalem for this feast, their hearts were filled with joy and excitement as singing and laughter could be heard from their caravans. They couldn't wait to get there.

When they arrived in Jerusalem, they began making their "huts" or "shelters" just like the Lord had instructed them. When the feast arrived, thousands of leafy green huts lined the streets of Jerusalem and dotted the surrounding fields and countryside.

God instructed them to build huts to remind them of how He had provided for them and sheltered them as they made their way through the wilderness from Egypt to the Promised Land. But that wasn't the only reason God told them to do it.

What they were living in, in the wilderness, was temporary. Soon they would reach their final destination, the Promised Land. It points to a past and future time for us who know the Lord—the Lord tabernacled among us on this earth so that we can tabernacle with Him forever without tears or death or pain or sorrow! That's what our hearts joyously long for. We long for a day when righteousness rules and where we will dwell with the Lord of Hosts and with the Lamb in Heaven eternally.

SHeLTeRS CeLeBRatioN

The Festival of Shelters occurs 5 days after the Day of Atonement. Pick a day around this time (maybe like a Friday night) and make this a joyous, memory-filled night. As a matter of fact, make this as much fun as you can because you are celebrating two events:

(1) **God coming to this earth in the person of Jesus** to tabernacle among us so that He could live the righteous life that we could never attain and die the sacrificial death, because of sin, that should have been ours! God came to live among His people. (This is actually the correct time for Christmas to be celebrated, and it now makes perfect sense!)

(2) **Christ-followers, forever in the presence of God in Heaven.** God's home is now among His people!

Celebrate in this way:

Camping—you are going to participate in your very own "shelter" celebration by setting up your camping tent in your backyard. (Make sure when you set it up that you have a clear view of your house in sight).

Heaven Food—*"What is Heaven food,"* you might be asking? Heaven food is the kind of food you would expect to find in Heaven, where you can eat everything you want and all you want of it and it doesn't get stuck around your waist. That kind of food! It is a night of eating everyone's favorites.

Gifts—give gifts to your kids. Wrap them up and surprise them with some presents. After all, this is the true time to celebrate Christmas, God coming to earth! Let them know that this is a special time and a joyous time that all points to God coming to live among us and us, one day, living in Heaven forever with Him.

Talk about God coming to live on this earth with us.

Read together the Christmas story in its proper context. Take turns reading the Scriptures.

At that time the Roman emperor, Augustus, decreed that a census should be taken throughout the Roman Empire. ² (This was the first census taken when Quirinius was governor of Syria.) ³ All returned to their own ancestral towns to register for this census. ⁴ And because Joseph was a descendant of King David, he had to go to Bethlehem in Judea, David's ancient home. He traveled there from the village of Nazareth in Galilee. ⁵ He took with him Mary, to whom he was engaged, who was now expecting a child.

⁶ And while they were there, the time came for her baby to be born. ⁷ She gave birth to her firstborn son. She wrapped him snugly in strips of cloth and laid him in a manger, because there was no lodging available for them.

8 That night there were shepherds staying in the fields nearby, guarding their flocks of sheep. 9 Suddenly, an angel of the Lord appeared among them, and the radiance of the Lord's glory surrounded them. They were terrified, 10 but the angel reassured them. "Don't be afraid!" he said. "I bring you good news that will bring great joy to all people. 11 The Savior—yes, the Messiah, the Lord—has been born today in Bethlehem, the city of David! 12 And you will recognize him by this sign: You will find a baby wrapped snugly in strips of cloth, lying in a manger." 13 Suddenly, the angel was joined by a vast host of others—the armies of heaven—praising God and saying, 14 "Glory to God in highest heaven, and peace on earth to those with whom God is pleased."

15 When the angels had returned to heaven, the shepherds said to each other, "Let's go to Bethlehem! Let's see this thing that has happened, which the Lord has told us about." 16 They hurried to the village and found Mary and Joseph. And there was the baby, lying in the manger. 17 After seeing him, the shepherds told everyone what had happened and what the angel had said to them about this child. 18 All who heard the shepherds' story were astonished, 19 but Mary kept all these things in her heart and thought about them often. 20 The shep-

herds went back to their flocks, glorifying and praising God for all they had heard and seen. It was just as the angel had told them.

Why celebrate the birth of Christ during the Feast of Shelters? It makes the most sense. If you look at the Biblical timeline of events surrounding His birth, you understand that Jesus was born sometime in September, on or around the Feast of Shelters.

How do we know this? For one, Caesar would not have jeopardized this census by calling for dangerous travel during the harsh winter months. For another, the text also says that shepherds were tending to their flocks outside in the field. Again, this is something that wouldn't have been done in the rainy, wintry Judean months.

The point is not to fixate on a date since one is not given in the New Testament, but on a purpose. Why did Jesus come? To tabernacle among us!

And the Word became flesh and tabernacled among us. We looked upon His glory, the glory of the one and only from the Father, full of grace and truth. (John 1:14 TLV)

Why did He tabernacle and make His home among us?

God was in Christ, reconciling the world to himself, no longer counting people's sins against them. And he gave us this wonderful message of reconciliation. 20 So we are Christ's ambassadors; God is making his appeal through us. We speak for Christ when we plead, "Come back to God!" [21] *For God made Christ, who never sinned, to be the offering for our sin, so that we could be made right with God through Christ. (2 Corinthians 5:19-21 NLT)*

Jesus being born on the Feast of Shelters is a clear picture of the Gospel; God taking on human skin, coming to live among us, in order to redeem us from the curse of the law!

Talk next about us living in Heaven with Him. Take turns reading these Scriptures:

Then I saw a new heaven and a new earth, for the old heaven and the old earth had disappeared. And the sea was also gone. [2] *And I saw the holy city, the new Jerusalem, coming down from God out of heaven like a bride beautifully dressed for her husband.* [3] *I heard a loud shout from the throne, saying, "Look, God's home is now among his people! He will live with them, and they will be his people. God himself will be with them.* [4] *He will wipe every tear from their eyes, and there will be no more death or sorrow or crying or pain. All these things are gone forever."* [5] *And the one sitting on the throne said, "Look, I am making everything new!" And then he said to me, "Write this down, for what I tell you is trustworthy and true."* [6] *And he also said, "It is fin-*

ished! I am the Alpha and the Omega—the Beginning and the End. To all who are thirsty I will give freely from the springs of the water of life. ⁷ All who are victorious will inherit all these blessings, and I will be their God, and they will be my children. (Revelation 21:1-7 NLT)

I saw no temple in the city, for the Lord God Almighty and the Lamb are its temple. ²³ And the city has no need of sun or moon, for the glory of God illuminates the city, and the Lamb is its light. ²⁴ The nations will walk in its light, and the kings of the world will enter the city in all their glory. ²⁵ Its gates will never be closed at the end of day because there is no night there. ²⁶ And all the nations will bring their glory and honor into the city. ²⁷ Nothing evil will be allowed to enter, nor anyone who practices shameful idolatry and dishonesty—but only those whose names are written in the Lamb's Book of Life. (Revelation 21:22-27 NLT)

Then the angel showed me a river with the water of life, clear as crystal, flowing from the throne of God and of the Lamb. ² It flowed down the center of the main street. On each side of the river grew a tree of life, bearing twelve crops of fruit, with a fresh crop each month. The leaves were used for medicine to heal the nations. ³ No longer will there be a curse upon anything. For the throne of God and of the Lamb will be there, and his servants will worship him. ⁴ And they will see his face, and his name will be written on their foreheads. ⁵ And there will be no night there—no need for lamps or sun—for the Lord God will shine on them. And they will reign forever and ever. ⁶ Then the angel said to me, "Everything you have heard and seen is trustworthy and true. The Lord God, who inspires his prophets, has sent his angel to tell his servants what will happen soon. (Revelation 22:1-6 NLT)

God made His home on this earth in the person of Jesus. In the near future, God's home will be among His people for all eternity as we dwell with the Lord and He with us forever and ever!

After the Day of Atonement, where we will all stand before God to be judged, God will wipe away all tears from His children's eyes. There will be no more sorrow for the former things. It will be an eternity of rejoicing as we dwell in the presence of the Lord.

Connect the dots for your kids. Say to them, *"This is why we are having this much fun and eating this food and giving each other gifts. We are celebrating the fact that God was born and came to live among us in order to rescue us from the curse of sin."*

Say this also to your children, *"We are also having this much fun to remind us of the future day when God will wipe away every tear, and we will dwell in the house of the Lord forever and ever."*

Lastly, tell them about the tent. Say to them, *"God came to temporarily tabernacle among us in the person of Jesus. He did so to make a way for us to be with Him in Heaven. In the same way, we are made, not for this life but for the life to come. Our earthly body, our earthly tent, is wearing out and getting old. We look forward to the day when our earthly body will be exchanged for a Heavenly one!"*

Say also to them, *"Just as this tent, this tabernacle that we are sleeping in tonight is not our real home, so this earth is not our real home."*

Say to them, *"This tent is not our home. There's our home."* (Point to your house).

Say to them again, *"That house is not our home. Heaven is our home* (point to the sky). *Let us never forget that."*

Enjoy the rest of the feast knowing that Heaven awaits those who know the Lord! All tears will be wiped away, and there will be eternal joy in the presence of the Lord! Play games together! Watch movies together! Spend time together, and enjoy this celebratory time!

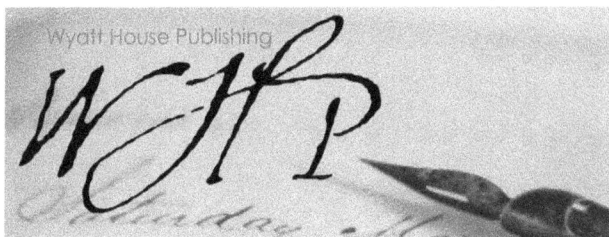

www.ingramcontent.com/pod-product-compliance
Lightning Source LLC
Chambersburg PA
CBHW021509090426
42739CB00007B/534